Wordsongs

Unfold.
♡ Laura West

LAURA WEST

ISBN: 978-1-64184-311-9

This book is a reminder that you are not alone in your humanity.

Stop.
Pause.
Breathe.
Feel.

I don't know if art would exist without pain, but I do know that creation makes pain have a purpose.
And sometimes, creation is my healing.
I also know that living a life focused on honesty and integrity has allowed me to create more beauty than living a life of pretending ever did.
It's messy, but it's real.

Pain. Suffering. Loss. Grief. Loneliness.
Beauty. Peace. Grace. Love. Hope.
Alchemy. Paradox. Contradictions. Complexity.

We share our humanity.

This is my dream.
This is my offering.

Contents

Unfold 1

My Art is Love 3

Spring 5

Beautiful Surprise 7

A Woman 8

The North 10

Canvas 12

Alchemy 13

Wasted Time 15

Water 17

Human 19

Love Is Dumb 22

Breathless 24

Neither You Nor I 26

The Death Of Me 28

Inside of Me 30

Being in Love 31

Mixing Magic 32

The Moon 34

You. 36

Intercepted by Ghosts 38

Made A Hurricane. 41

A Vow 43

Pain I Can Sustain 45

Storyteller 47

Pure and Untamed 48

Fabricated Angel 49

Heresy 51

In This Moment 53

Beautiful Still 55

Stuck in Time 57

The Best is Yet to Come 59

Unfold

unfold

please don't find your space in hiding
i know it's terrifying
the world is unrelenting
it's hard to trust what you're presenting

unfold

trust me
it is beautiful out here
the truth we're celebrating
the connection we're anticipating
the life we are creating

unfold

you will not find perfection
still, you will face rejection
but all these walls that we build don't
provide protection
come join this ragamuffin. human.
collection.
it might feel like your dissection

but beautiful, you don't need perfection

unfold

you are enough
just as you are
honest and raw
broken and beautiful
let's celebrate
you

unfold

My Art is Love

i would work for you, cry for you, lay down my life
for you
i would go through drudgery, grindstone,
and embrace any toil
lay it all on the line only to watch my dreams foiled

my art is love.

i would surrender it all, live the life of risk
for you
i would acknowledge liability as opportunity
and uncertainty as possibility
forego circumstance and fortune,
wagering a life of futility

my art is love.

i would wage war for you, turn the
world upside down for you
i would battle all that should be,
composing a holy mess
pandemonium is my peace,
misconception my success

my art is love.

i would endure for you, yield to you, wave my white
flag for you
i would dismantle cruelty and revenge never seek
my life is a design of invention,
free falling into your mystique

my art is love.

Spring

for the ones who feel dizzy and are starting to fall
the ones who feel helpless, like they've lost it all
for the ones who keep speaking but have no voice
the ones who lost hope and feel like they don't have a
choice

for the ones who feel crazy and
misunderstood
the ones who aren't getting what fairly they
should
for the ones who keep trying but can't gain
traction
the ones who cannot believe
another's reaction

for the ones who feel lonely with
no one by their side
the ones who keep looking for a safe
place to hide
for the ones who keep seeking for
unselfish gain
the ones who look around and almost
nothing remains

for the ones who feel inadequate; is it ever
enough?

the ones who life treats just a little too rough
for the ones who keep loving and get hate in return
the ones whose only possessions are lessons learned

for the ones who feel disconnected while reaching out
the ones who have no voice, no matter how loud
they shout
for the ones who keep going no matter what the cost
the ones who can't count everything that they've lost

for the ones who will have a hard time believing
my words
someday you will feel as free as the birds
because freedom and flying and love don't cost a thing
and after the winter, always there is spring

Beautiful Surprise

don't use love as oppression
and fear to withhold
please stop honoring aggression
leaving no space to behold
the beauty around us
won't you please let it rise?
let the truth surround us
put away your disguise
and may life become
the most beautiful surprise

A Woman

tell me
what does it look like to be a woman?

but don't tell me about having it all
as i try to write
but i can't breathe from the guilt gripping my chest
as i try to leave
but my kids scream and my heart shatters
not only because of their unmet wants
but also because of

mine

as i try to be
let me be
not overtaken by
the pressure

so, tell me

i can be a mom and nurture?
i can tame my passion?
i can shut up or shut down
afraid of what i might
become

but what if i am more afraid of what i
don't become?

because what about my other "options"

OR

i can be strong
intelligent
driven

OR

i can be wild and
free
so, tell me
you want me to pursue
until it makes you uncomfortable
you want me to love
what you tell me to love
you want me to feel
what you can hold in the palm of your hand
nothing more.
nothing less.

why do you get to tell me what it means to be a
woman?

The North

i have lived in the north but not responsibly

thoughtlessly
ironically

i let him put his cold hands on every inch of me
and not just my body
the ice gripped my soul
i lost all control
and dreams of being made whole

rugged and stark

i fumbled through the cold dark
until i was ready to embark
to greater depths of the expanse

because the north was just one
direction
the first to offer protection
but his limits led to destruction

because one part is never the whole

the north held a lofty promise

but alone could not be flawless
dishonoring my internal compass
defined by
disconnection and loss

i entered the north as a novice
but i left as a

goddess

yet sorrow remained
that the north was not my home

Canvas

i am fear
i am fire
the object of desire
i hold dreams
i hold schemes
everything lies in between

i am alone
i am alive
the chronicles of an archive
i go deep
i rise
my soul a ceaseless surprise

i invoke
i inspire
the object of desire
i create elegance
i create madness
my life is a canvas

Alchemy

let it be light
be you
be free
let your love be confetti
for you and for me
let it be light
there is too much heavy
they'll drag you down with their pain
wobbly
unsteady
let it be light

let it be grief
feel your pain
be a mess
let your heart hold the distress
of the world's unkindness
let it be grief
we all get lost in sadness
don't rush yourself to convalesce
healing
it will come
let it be grief

let it be alchemy

take both
make them gold
find the depths of what you can hold
let all that can be unfold
let it be alchemy
allow your story to be told
and in the beauty behold
mystery
a revolutionary
let it be alchemy

Wasted Time

i need to start pacing
my wasted time
they all want verses
i'll give them a line

take them higher
than the moon
watch them fall
watch me swoon

reckless like fire
crazy like desire
stand back and admire
baby, we were live wire

relentless like loneliness
can't take any more of this
lust leads to weakness
surrendering my genius

brutal like retaliation
i am only your temptation
not your salvation
when did love become amputation?

so i need to start pacing

my wasted time
because they all want versus
i keep giving them lines

taking it all as he leaves
slamming doors in my heart
all this wasted time
is tearing me apart

Water

i am water

gentle healing that will reawaken your soul
but i will cut you like a knife
my strength can give you strength
my life can give you life
i can blur your vision
or i can make things clear
i can be the death of you
drowning you or all your fears

do not disrespect me
i run wild
i run free
i am comfortable in stillness
alive in adversity
because with me there is peace
but that might threaten your
worldview
either way, don't look my way
start by looking within you

someday, you will run back to me
ready to see your true reflection
but my compass isn't clarity

i'll point you in all directions
because i have found love and wisdom
in the process of my flow
i am not for the weak of heart
or those not willing to dive below
the typical
the surface
the simple
easy understanding
if you seek the path of least resistance
you'll find meaning too demanding

but when you learn to come alive in fire
when you learn to stand tall in the storm
you will learn what it means to fight for love
and what it means to be reborn

Human

i miss moments
i know this
my mind
makes me blind
to the sunset
but i won't forget
all the beauty
that i see

the family swimming
the mysterious and curious rainbow
the fat seagull catching bugs
how the sand feels between
my toes
the little boys splashing in
the waves
the old men fishing

they're all waiting

creating
a moment
i know it
and i try not to show it
that romance remains

untamed

say my name
choose me
then they do
and i run

back to the moon
but then it's late afternoon
and i start to remember
how i have too much to miss
i can't take any more of this
i'm trying to get to
places that don't exist

my mind, insatiable
a wild animal
out of control

then
i notice the sun has set
the timing
out of my control
everyone's leaving
i am watching them go
and i'm stuck in a moment
i know it

maybe it's regret
maybe i'll never forget
to remember how to connect
and keep missing
more than moments
because i don't even feel
human

Love Is Dumb

let's be honest
love is dumb

maybe my heart beats faster
than a drum
maybe my thoughts are tangled up like string
and suddenly
you're my everything

maybe my stomach is full of butterflies
but my big brown eyes
see straight through your lies

and even though i know
you're only an addiction
you become
my greatest affliction

logically
it all makes sense
i don't need
more evidence

i am destroyed by desire
burnt by my own fire

we complicate the simple
lost in our egos
and in this world of obsession
everything we want is impossible

but can we just be honest
this isn't love
because love isn't dumb

and as much as i understand
the equation of dysfunction
i can't stop my heart
from this incessant malfunction

but it's no longer
pretty
exciting
or fun
so, let's be honest
love is dumb

Breathless

breathless

like moments of ecstasy
or moments of tragedy
tear stained face
or hoping you're my destiny

shadows of horror
or hope resonating
fueling the flames
of the life we're creating

rushing like waves
overtaking me

dreadfully

desperately

looking for a remedy

hope. precariously.
alone. therapy.

whatever it takes

i give you my pleasantries
but i'm filled with perplexity

tentatively

rebelliously

seeking equity

yet i'm left
breathlessly

still breathing

Neither You Nor

i can wake you up
blow your mind like a bomb
make you feel more
than the greatest love song

i can show you parts of life
you've never seen
i can sell you all
my wildest dreams

and neither you nor i
will remember if they're yours
or mine
and neither you nor i
will know if i'm yours or mine

i can fall into you
just like you're falling in love
you will believe that i
fit you like a glove

you won't feel loneliness
you'll feel understood
how can your life possibly

be this good?

and neither you nor i
can make you mine
and neither you nor i
will know if i'm yours or mine

but what i'm waiting for
what i'm hoping for
what i'm praying for
is that someday i'm yours

but before i can know
before we can grow
before dreams come true
make me feel like i do

because i've been alone
for far too long
i've felt loneliness deeper
than the greatest sad song

and i want this to be
i want to be free
i want to feel how you feel
i want something real

but until i do

i can't give myself to you

The Death Of Me

the gravity of it all hits me like being buried alive
i'm watching the dirt fall, not even surprised

you hurt me. you betrayed me.
unable to care
about anyone but you
did you even realize we were there?

i looked to you. they looked to you.

flesh of your flesh

but you grabbed a shovel
i tried to make do with what
was left

but now i lie alone in bed
being buried alive
living my pain again
for the thousandth time

and as you shovel more dirt
i'm shoveling too
but i keep falling behind
i could never keep up with you

your wicked schemes
overtake my wildest dreams

how do you keep winning?
it keeps my head spinning.

so, i'll cry myself to sleep again
not because of you but the pain
of human existence
of what little remains

and i'll get up in the morning
and keep shoveling your doom off me

because the only choice is to be relentless

i'm going to be free
even if it's the death of me

Inside of Me

i'm sick of waking up to tragedies
when i'm dreaming of making melodies
because i'm starting to see that you and me
can't live up to my fantasies

you keep running in another direction
seeking the devil's protection
because all your comfortable distractions
are only counterfeit assassination

but you're choosing to be blind
now, i can't escape my mind
and in life, love, there's no rewind
we're all living these lives that
we've designed

while pointing our fingers lazily
in any direction that points away
from me
because do we really want to see?

do you really want to see?

i'm done looking for a guarantee

outside of me

Being in Love

it's fated
full of mystery

outdated
older than you and me

connected
like constellations

in the nighttime sky

there is lightning
in hearts

it's frightening
this art

there's no fighting
the force

of being in love

Mixing Magic

you have darkness in your eyes
i have light inside my heart
you are madness, babe, it's tragic
my life is a work of art

i have wildness in my eyes
you have love inside your heart
i am madness, babe, it's tragic
please make me your work of art

darkness falls
you're making melodies
i'm a mess
but you can have what's
left of me
i'm alone
my mind's a tragedy
you're surrounded
always eluding gravity

you paint pictures in your mind
i am lost in a sea of words
you're a catastrophe; i'm in constant
reverie
let's fly higher than the birds

i fight battles in my head
you paint peace with your two hands
i'm a catastrophe, you're lost in reverie
while i dream of you being my man

darkness falls
you're making melodies
i'm a mess
but you can have what's left of me
i'm alone
my mind's a tragedy
you're surrounded
always eluding gravity

you saw me
i saw you
i was dreaming about you
before you knew
now you're the one making me smile
let's stay here for a little while

you didn't know it
i couldn't see it
please never stop, baby, i admit
you're the one i can't quit
let's keep mixing magic

The Moon

the moon reminds me that whatever we have to offer
today is enough

sometimes...

we can be fully reflected
seen in all our great beauty

and sometimes...

we disappear into the
abyss of darkness

sometimes...

we are overtaken

sometimes...

we simply must retreat for our own
greatness
our own desire

we must create our own space

but we're still there

we are still here

all that we are remains even when it can't be seen by
others

You

you

give me butterflies
make my heart beat faster
my eyes
tell the truth
you're the one that i'm after

you

give me hopelessly romantic
fantasies
make me feel like i have
all the things
i have seen...
in my dreams

you

give me desire
to return
to desires
forgotten
dreams i killed
buried in coffins

you

give me depth
resurrecting
so much death
redemption
i'm digging up
all the dreams that
i left

you

give me reassurance
my dreams are
becoming
reality
because i will give you
all that is left of me

you

take away rhythm
and rhyme
make my head spin

time

please go faster
be the one that i'm after

Intercepted by Ghosts

maybe that's what makes us wild
this fire in our souls
we are lovers
we are fighters
intercepted by ghosts
maybe that's what makes us crazy
this sparkle in our eyes
we see all the things invisible
a beautiful surprise

we wake up with words on our tongues
and music on our minds
we have nowhere to belong, and
we have nothing but time
on the outskirts of humanity, we
frolic with souls
drawn to something deeper,
intercepted by ghosts

we are alive in imagination; creation is
our fire
we have nowhere to belong, overflowing
with desire

in the water, under the moon, we come alive
because it takes the depths for souls to collide

we sleep awake in our dreams and fall asleep
when awake
we run back to our dreams, to the worlds we create
in the worlds that we create, we frolic with souls
drawn to madness and magic, intercepted by ghosts

we are dead in deception, truth is our fire
why can't you see that we belong? wait... be inspired.
in our death and decay, our greatness is known
we live a different kind of death, only captivated
by bones

maybe that's what makes us wild
this fire in our souls
we are lovers
we are fighters
intercepted by ghosts
maybe that's what makes us crazy
this sparkle in our eyes
we see all the things invisible
a beautiful surprise

we are born with spirits in our lungs, addiction in
our souls
we have adoration in our brains and hearts made
of gold

in the quiet, sacred spaces, we frolic with souls
dancing with spirits, intercepted by ghosts

we are alive in obsession; creation is our fire
we belong everywhere there is passion or desire
in the water, under the sun, we come alive
because it takes the light for souls to collide

our death will be our greatness; someday, you will see
we have everything to offer, our complex humanity
despite your unawareness, we frolicked with your soul
drawn to perfection and light, intercepted by ghosts

we are dead in our body, alive in legacy
because sometimes it takes time to appreciate beauty
in our death and decay, our greatness is known
we die a different kind of death, finally not alone

maybe that's what makes us wild
this fire in our souls
we are lovers
we are fighters
intercepted by ghosts
maybe that's what makes us crazy
this sparkle in our eyes
we see all the things invisible
a beautiful surprise

Made A Hurricane

i never could come in silently
quietly
neatly

i won't be your tidy
your sweet, classy lady

i was made a hurricane
entering with disruption
unafraid of destruction
but if you would let me
i would be your redemption

i have wild eyes
an untamed heart
a beautiful soul

don't think you're making me whole

underestimate me
in time, you will see
it's probably best
to let me be me

if you're afraid of beauty
afraid of connection
afraid of love
afraid of destruction

take your eyes and your heart
and find a pretty distraction
but now that you've tasted and seen
you know that she'll never be me

A Vow

desperation
temptation
to run

survival
it's vital
to some

resurrection
my dissection
to hope

reality
vitality
a tightrope

stumbling
falling
i break

i pray the Lord my soul to take

the past
the future
right now

hanging
in the balance of
a vow

Pain I Can Sustain

i often live wasting time
by creating messes in my mind
suffering sufferings that are not real
fighting endless fights to simply heal

i live in detrimental fantasies
married to fear that may never leave
overpowered from living so unempowered
jaded by loves that too quickly sour

i often live wasting time
coming alive, alone, in words
that rhyme
writing the things that haunt
my brain

insanity is making me insane

i question questions others never ask
haunted by thoughts that blow up
their masks
both the bomb and the beauty that
remains

insanity is making me insane

so, i made friends with the messes in my mind
so, i no longer live wasting time

presence
patience
my masterpiece

beginning to come alive in the love that frees

releasing
detrimental fantasies

all the things that are not for me

i asked; i pleaded,
"what is mine to do?"

then i packed my bags,
and i left you

because things are often not what they seem
my eyes look past the empty dreams

insanity still makes me insane

but i have chosen the
pain i can sustain

Storyteller

i have learned to thrive in empty space
where most don't dare to go
the barren land, no longer green
where roots tangle in messes
below

green fades, and hope is dissipating
at least to the naked eye
but if you dare look deeper,
it's still covered in massive, endless
skies

beyond the brokenness and death
the clouds overtake the moon
at night
always darkness threatens
but nothing can diminish our true
light

it shines along the outer lines
awake on the fringes with the border
dwellers
so in its stubbornness and fierceness
nature remains my favorite
storyteller

Pure and Untamed

i remain both
dove and serpent
no matter what you see

my virtue is authentic
my desires
rampant and free

you may only honor
the dove
but the serpent will remain

complexity is my home
paradoxically
pure and untamed

Fabricated Angel

i could never be the angel in your house
though i always sought to be
more quiet
selfless
all for you
diminishing
what's left of me

i waited
weighted
i wore white

though blackness oozed
infected

intuition became my disease
existence the sum of all that i
rejected

i lied while i lied
pretending
truer a martyr than your savior

my innocence
my prison

the imperfect perfection of my behavior

i became the siren in your house
though i couldn't help but be
true as the waves that destroyed
your rocky charade out in the sea

it's well
i swell up
overflowing

like rising after death

you killed me but i killed me too
uncertain who forced my final breath

i tried while i tried

pretending

more real than
divine or beautiful

my destruction became my lesson

i will never be your
fabricated angel

Heresy

tonight, i'm feeling reckless
thinking of ways to find some justice
maybe i'm a little bit senseless
from pretending to be helpless

swallowing the truth for far too long
i know i'm right
i know you're wrong
you won't stop
so headstrong

but we both know that
i don't belong

underneath your pile of ashes
i'll burn
you
grab the matches
and as the light continually flashes
in your eyes
i see the passion

there's no need to be dramatic
you always knew that
i was magic

but frantic so you panic
now we're left being nostalgic

we keep trying so desperately
to amount to more than wild chemistry
but we both knew all along that
you and me
are the greatest type of
heresy

In This Moment

sometimes
i want to go back
to before i knew
the calamity
of losing you
innocence vanished
generations forgotten
i look back on my dreams
and find that they're rotten

sometimes
i want to move forward
to when i will find
the perfect one
who will make me blind
to the pain of my past
betrayal in my blood
pumping through my veins
uncontained like a flood

never
i want to stay here
fully awake to the time
the in between
that makes us rewind
to the long lost suffering

to the future, bleak
so forgive my soul in this moment
for i am weak

Beautiful Still

i'll find my way back home
it won't be far
i have seen the lights
i have seen the stars
i have lived with the renegades
i have walked through flames
i have been baptized in blood
by those who don't know my name

i'll find my way back home
it might be too far
i have seen the lights
i have been the stars
i have been left alone
in the darkest alley at night
when i was most broken
i had to invent my own light

because the ones who should have
the ones who said that they care
couldn't lay their eyes on me
so i watched them stare
off in the distance
to a castle on a hill

gasping for breath
i'm drowning still

and in the depths of despair
in the agonizing darkness
in the brutality of alone
in the chaos of stress

i found my way back home
it is never too far
to find your light
to dwell with the stars
because maybe we all can't fit
in a castle on a hill

but maybe in misunderstanding
we are beautiful still

Stuck in Time

i hope this isn't it

the lonely nights
the loneliness
the desperate longing
for someone to kiss
to call my own
he'll want me too
he'll make me forget
about me and you

i hope this isn't it

the beautiful silence
mad determination
relentlessly running
to a question mark destination
to find a way
to escape the chaos
that exists in my brain
elusive homeostasis

i hope this isn't it

the lost innocence
will i hope again?
dreadfully, i fear
i'm my only friend
to trust, have faith
to calm my fears
who can withstand
my ocean of tears

i hope this isn't it

the haunting hope
that i'll breathe soon
the growing faith
the rhythmic moon
i know the truth
i honor the waves
the only way this is it
is if we become slaves

to the comfort
the drudgery
the old rhythm and rhyme
so do me a favor
and don't get stuck in time

The Best is Yet to Come

when all seems lost
and life is a bag of bones at your feet

when you feel forgotten
and survival is retreat

when brokenness comes
and darkness overtakes you like winter

when you are alone
and can't find the glimmer

of
hope
love
connection
or
grace

draw plus signs on your heart
put a smile on your face

or maybe a frown
maybe some tears

whatever it takes for you to stay here

because pain is threatening
alone is deadening

but

the worst is over

and the best is yet to come

...the best is yet to come...